Miracle and Believers

Jackie Bynum

outskirts
press

Table of Contents

———◆———

The Best Seller of the Year.

———◆———

My Life as a Living Miracle

IT STARTS FROM the womb. A child is born, and we should not forget the reality of what is about to happen throughout the coming lifetime. We forget that we all are born sinners, and the question is "does the parent or parents know that they are about to deliver a sinner or a Satan?" *We as mothers should* vociferously read, pray, talk, and teach the infant while the child is in the womb, and throughout pregnancy but, of course, that is just the beginning. A mother being a parent has this job to do for the rest of that child's life. The child will have stumbling blocks, and will be challenged, and you will learn right from wrong along the way. Now you should be focusing on the winning prize of giving birth to your unborn child and teaching the child about the right way and praying they won't go wrong. After birth you realize that you should have done this even before birth. If not, then there will be consequences and repercussions along the way. Don't do wrong things; learn to do right.

Submitting yourself to God means that you have agreed to follow His way for you to have a better life and it's not by force. It's a choice you make on your own. When you do so, then God gives you the strength to resist the temptation and the taunting of the Enemy. Now that you have learned about your higher power, the devil will flee in time; but knowing that Jesus is your rock and having a relationship with Him means that you will have to deal with your decisions or wrongdoings or "rightdoings" before and after death. There's no perfect person on earth; if we were perfect then we would already be in heaven. This means you will pay throughout your life and you will reap what you sow during a life span of time that you can't get around. Just think of decades of trying to learn how to live on earth. But you will always have options and choices to make.

And the choices you make become your life. The options are big and wide but the choices will reflect on your future and most definitely your child's life too. You must make wise choices for yourself and for a child of yours and others.

After a child is born, what a miracle, but while the infant is in the mother's womb the mothers should rub and hold their stomach every day. Mothers should talk, pray, and read to their infants as the child develops in the womb, and as you should know, keeping a balanced diet is a must. A balanced diet includes fruits, vegetables, nuts and grains, also plenty of rest, exercise, and happiness all around you. Life involves showing love and giving it in return. Another thing is praying over the child and singing to the child too.

Once you get into the habit of doing this every day, it will become normal as you and your infant grow together. This will make a happy baby who grows to be a happy child. You guys will grow together and will learn lessons through challenges that can benefit along the way. If a parent or parents don't start early then they will miss the best part of growing up. You can let life pass you by and miss out on your child's learning from day one, meaning things like "Don't touch the stove, it's hot, you will get burned", and "Stay away from the stairs, you'll fall and get hurt."

Things like that become a silent approach for life, and the message that you have learned at an early age sticks and becomes normal and now you're learning how to crawl before you can walk. Sometimes, as a person, you have steps to take and taking them is a choice. A choice of the knowledge of knowing right from wrong, now as a child with no knowledge this could be very hard. Now, where are moms and dads and are they on the same page, or did they forget that their job never ends? And do they know that they have to work overtime all the time. This is the period in a child's life when the child needs discipline and maybe gets spanked a lot. At certain moments the child may think momentarily that no one loves them, but real loving parents hurt every time they whip the child and feel bad about disciplining their child. They may cry with the child. I believe that it's a good thing to cry with your child so the child will know that it hurts the parents as much as it hurts them.

Sickness is something you may be born with or it may occur along the way and may take time to recover--only time will tell.

Now a child is in puberty and starting to smell themselves. They appear to be listening yet don't act or they seem to become hard of hearing. Puberty starts around age eleven through seventeen. Everyone is unique so that means different strokes for different folks. Teenagers are trying to find themselves and their way on their own. This is the time when the parent needs to pray more, teach more, and most definitely listen more. Most of the time a parent is also trying to learn for themselves and grow too. The parents are looking for new tools to help the child and themselves. This process is hard and can become harmful without clear direction.

Teenagers can feel lost, disturbed, disappointed, unloved, and impossible to deal with, because their hormones are developing and they are in a rage. This is like letting them go out into the world and praying that they make the best of it and hoping that they come back as the girl or the boy that left out the door too early. They don't know if they want to be a girl or a boy neither. This is why as parents we shouldn't ever stop praying, teaching and preaching. The love is still there and a child needs more attention now than ever before.

All parents have big expectations for their child and want the best for their future, but it doesn't always turn out that way. Teenagers, this doesn't mean it can't end in success but making a tight left turn means you will end up on the wrong side of the fence and it could land you in jail for robbing, stealing, drugs, and may result in prosecution.

You won't graduate and you won't go to college right away, because now you have to start all over and it will be harder and take longer to become a doctor, a judge, an attorney or the president of the United States, or some job in repair or manufacturing. But it may take longer than if you just stayed out of trouble. And faith without works is dead.This mess will lower your expectations for a healthy future. And now you hold your head up like your nose is bleeding. You think that you're a bigger person now because you made it to the big house, the wrong house, making all the left turns and not listening to your parents. Now you're older and you must pay heed to the teachers and your godly inner self.

If you're in prolonged trouble, you need prayer now and lots of it. You'll find time to pray and will be hoping to God that your loved ones are praying too. You've got to pray for help from up above and all around. Now you have to tell someone, cause now you need them. You need a listener, a preacher, and you're asking everyone and anyone to come and get you out of jail.

My mom told me that if I ever land to jail don't call her and I never did. I just prayed not to do it again and cried that I would never go back. We must all remember that we are born sinners and we have to learn the right from the wrong. It should come straight out of the womb, learning right from wrong. You may come to the rude realization that maybe you missed it or maybe it wasn't there.

When you hear that your child has done something wrong, the first thing you think of is I should've, would've, could've–or how did this happen when I used to spank and cry with them? Maybe I should've spent more time with them. Now the child is grown and having all these problems. How does that make you feel? O Lord, where did I go wrong, what has happened to my child? And now you have to hold your head up like your nose is bleeding, and the first thing a parent thinks is "What do I do now? Once you ask, you will receive cause the Lord will show and tell though part of you wants to cry. Still, you know it was the choice that a child makes by turning left when they should've stayed right. Now you wish you were back in church—a place you should've never left. You've got to begin praying down on your knees for the Lord's forgiveness and to make this go away, but the judge says different.

The parents always think that it's their fault, and sometimes it is. Good parents are hard workers; good parents spend time with their child in school activities help with homework, and teach the child how to pray. It's a very big job to constantly be aware of their whereabouts and what they're saying out of their mouth and to others. You must also know who they're listening to and who's really giving them guidelines. Hopefully, they're not making foolish decisions on their own. Remember, the main thing is guidance and lots of prayers.

Praying to your God and praying with your child will help them and you to become better persons. No doubt, in our hearts we should know that prayer works and it's real.

Some people like to procrastinate about going to church and having a prayer room. Having two prayer rooms means one for the family to pray all together and the other one for you to spend time with the Lord. This is mandatory, some will get it right away and for others it may take more time to get it or they never get in tune with God's intentions in this world. It's a must that you find the time to teach and learn about your higher power. Miracles are a must and you have to do the basic works as well.

Folks can become a Johnny come lately in any message but I hear my Lord cry and I'm living proof of my successful journey. It's never too late to live your dreams. I must warn you, though, there will be stumbling blocks and devilish type people everywhere you go every day.

Going to church was a big thing in my family but it wasn't a must. I love going to church with my family. In our house it was Mom who said, "I'm going to church and whoever wants to go then get up and get dressed."

I went because I loved dressing up. And as I got older it became a choice; it wasn't mandatory. And it is a choice within you had to make. I chose to skip church because I'd only attended to dress up and pray for things that I wasn't taught to pray for. I never really knew how to pray and what to pray for and didn't know that it should be mandatory. Nevertheless, to be totally honest I would rather be at home watching television. I never really understood the Bible. And when I read it, I couldn't get nothing out of it. The words were understandable but not to my knowledge. I only learnt so little.

Being raised from a family of eight, I was the sixth child. I think my parents just slowed down and were exhausted when they got to me and my two younger brothers. The teaching and preaching became less, and some days Mom just didn't have time because her job wore her to a frazzle. And the little freedom that she'd found along the way she took up some entertainment for herself and took us every summer on vacation. We would go to Six Flags in Saint Louis or to Columbus, Ohio to visit her oldest brother who had as many kids as she did. The trips were a thriller and now that I'm older I understand that it was her way of showing her love for us, and keeping her head up so her nose wouldn't bleed.

As we grew older we became curious and our behaviors had gotten worse. Mom was still maintaining from the knowledge that she knew best and when the teaching the preaching, and the training lessened I should have still pursued it, but I didn't catch it so I moved on and and am still trying to understand my spiritual roots in order to move on in my life. My mom had divorced my sister and brothers father because he was very abusive. Then she started dating my father and, ouch, here I am. We lived the good and the bad. We were raised with two sets of parents and on my dad's side they all used to drink just as on my mom's side, but they were always fighting and some of them hated me. I knew it because of how they talked or treated me. And now I know deep in my heart that they sometimes tried to show love and discipline in a different manner from home and I believe that love is part of being a unified family, which you should never divide. Because my father's side loved to fight and some did drugs, I couldn't wait to get back home from my summer vacations with my dad. Dad had problems going on too but he always pretended a pretty picture and that's all I wanted to see when I went to visit. I truly don't know about my parents past family history or how we all became the persons we are. Thinking about my roots, occasionally I glimpse little bits and pieces. But, overall, the struggle was hard and still is. I loved my parents and I wish I had asked more questions or set and listened. I believe I had a blockage in my head from my sister and brother pushing me down when I was a baby. Sometimes my two other brothers would cut me with a razor and then fuss about who was to blame while I was crying and bleeding. After that incident my mom started taking me to work with her.

I started working with my mom at a young age. I think now that she did it to keep me away from my sister and brothers and, as I got older, to keep me off the streets. But I was only four years old and I remember riding in the stroller on the bus and arriving at the grocery store where she worked. I couldn't have been no more than five. I started working with her up until I was ten or eleven. Some school days and some weekends, I went to work with her and because I was the baby girl she would take me with her everywhere. I believe that my siblings hated it but I loved it. I didn't wanna stay home anyway and I think that she didn't want to leave me there with my older siblings, but some days she took them to work too. But out of all of us I was the one who Lightfoot loved the most. We would catch the bus to 1501 south Keeler Avenue in Chicago to a corner grocery store. I learned how to do a lot of things there, far as cutting meat, counting money, putting prices on canned goods and much more. Lightfoot lived in the back of the store with his sister, Mary, and one day he brought me a bank and we used to put money in it every night before I went home, and when Christmas came he would open the bank and give me all the money that was in it and tell me to go and buy stuff for my family. And his sister, Mary, would just smile. She wasn't a big talker—always quiet with a pleasant smile. They looked like they were old as dirt, but they loved me.

Lightfoot had only one daughter as far as I knew and she had two girls. One was my age and the other was younger than me, and when they came to visit once or twice a week it was like heaven–like my day off of work. We used to play around the store. Mostly just walking through the store and looking at everything and they was well trained and they was as pretty as I. I had fun whenever they came. Lightfoot used to take me to the White Sox games on Sundays, that is, if I went to work with my mom. I really started liking Sundays. But my mom didn't work every Sunday and she would take us to church on the Sundays that she didn't work. When Mr. Lightfoot took me to the White Sox game, he would drive his red car to the train station and we would leave the car and get on the train and once we got there we always had a soda pop, hot dogs and popcorn. This was another good day with my mom at work and another good memory of that time. I also didn't have to work that day and when we came back to the store, I was in dreamland dreaming of the wonderful time we shared that day. Then I would take a nap. Lightfoot knew that my mom was a good worker and he tried to help her any way he could and I loved him as if he was my boss too. But Lightfoot's store was robbed at least twice a month. And I was just in there as a child praying that no one gets hurt.

I would stamp food cans, put cans on the shelves, stack the pop coolers, drink all the soda pop and eat ice cream. I know now that's why I don't care for soda today. My mom used to let me sell the candy to the candy costumers. I learned how to count, and I learned how to not like soda pop at an early age.

After all those robberies, I felt like I didn't like Chicago anymore. I learned later that crime was everywhere and not just at the store we worked. Come to find out crime was all over the world and because I was very young I thought that it was just happening there in Chicago.

Now that I been working since I was a little girl, and am still working on something other than a nine to five job, I'm doing something else that's far bigger and better. Remember, you must never be defined by what someone tells you. Unkind words from others may push you in another direction–a direction that wasn't in your plan.

Folks need to understand what a person's been through and help them in any situation to learn how to treat others, even if you don't know about their past lifestyle. Whether they are ex-convicts or ex-drug addicts, you know there's always choices to make–good or bad. I've come to realize I can't try to fix everything and everyone. But you can find yourself and love yourself and your loved ones. While not forgetting how bad life was at one time, we must focus on to-day and tomorrow and not yesterday. Wash your hands in the blood, raise them in the holy Mary, and dry them in Christ's righteousness. I learned how to wash my hands in what I pray for, raise my hands for what I dream for, and I'm still learning how to dry them.

Dr. Martin Luther King had a dream of hope and a dream of some-day living in peace, but we fall short of his dream because we are not remembering the past of our ancestors and the big picture of their struggles. Life now involves knowing that there is something bigger than what you see and what you know. There's a supernatural miracle in this world which includes peace if you will only seek it with your heart. My theory is to believe in something higher and beyond my present and meditate on dreams of being equal and pray to help oth-ers to teach the love and peace of Christ. The government puts stuff out in the news and in the communities to evoke your emotions in regard to drugs and killings by the police to make us upset so we will retaliate and push harm on others. But we cannot focus on hatred and revenge against the police. That's not right and it's never the answer.

Humble yourself and pray; take one step backward and not for-ward to the energy that lies ahead. I decided to write about some-thing that folks need to hear and hopefully it will give them a better understanding. They must realize that they can begin learning at an early age and not wait until they're old as me to understand what it is to truly live. Do you know that you have to go through something at times to get to something else. I went through a lot to get to where I'm at today and I thank God that I made it this far. I did all kinds of crime. If you want to bring God into your life it has to be real.

Crime is contagious and it doesn't pay. You start doing things on your own. You'll get caught up in some mighty bad things--things like drugs and jail. I don't know why people imagine that if they're in the fast lane, and they made that left turn instead of the right one, they will never end up in jail or in the graveyard. There had to be a whole lot of praying for me, I mean not just me praying. I'm saying that there were somebodies other than me that were praying for my return. There's a God and there's a Holy Spirit and He's real.

I remember visiting the Indians in India, they always went to church and I remember them telling me to pray to my God all the time, and I went to church with them a time or two, and it was way different from the churches that I had attended throughout my life. They have a different kind of way to worship their God and the way they do it is much different from what I've ever known. I was so speechless and I wanted them to know my God. I felt so different and the differences in the language really made me feel blessed. When we left, I was more excited knowing that I didn't catch what they prayed about but eager to learn. But I knew if this was something I needed to learn then I must study. I also knew that the Lord is real. And it matters what God you serve. He's a mighty God and He's real as the day you're born, and as real as the fact that you need food for nourishing your body every day.

I found my miracle and my belief. One is to be able to write this message and to live to tell the story. I always believed that I was an educated person and I knew that I could do better someday. I liked a few things about school but I didn't like to go and, even in my drug addictions, I knew that there was something more about me than just looking good and hanging out with ballers. I also knew that God had other plans for me and he didn't just save me from all the bad wrongs I had done. But he saved me to realize what I had done to my kids and family.

Now I struggle for happiness and to make a difference. I was determined to finish something and my challenge was to stay in school no matter what and to find a church home no matter where, and that was what I did from state to state and from city to city. I was in school and in church. I have the faith and I have the beliefs and now I'm doing the work. I learned how to stay focused and pray. I know that there's something more powerful than myself and more powerful than anyone else.

I started out to be a cosmetologist. I went to the school alone while trying to get my GED on the side, but back then you didn't need a high school diploma or a GED to start beauty school and that was where I made my mistake. Because instead of me finishing school I decided that I wanted to learn about the streets too. So I hung out with the best of the high rollers and ballers, at least that was what I thought they were. I ended up on drugs, didn't finish nothing. I started and became a baller and a street runner, gambling, drinking, taking drugs to stay awake so I couldn't get to class on time. Finally I dropped out.

The streets seemed good to me and it was easier to run the streets than to study for a test. I was a sad baller cause every year it became harder and the baller part led me farther and farther from my dreams and far from my correct destination. This is what drugs can do to you and looking back on all those years that had passed me by I felt lost and disappointed. I found out that you can't do it by yourself--being on drugs and selling them too. I was trying to keep my high and knowing in the back of my head I was doing wrong and trying to make some right out of it. Sometimes you may think that you need a fix because of being hooked and whatever you take for your fix is an addiction. I been through hikes and some didn't involve using the same kind of drugs I was. The mind plays games all the time. A person can be hiking you up for a ride or a babysitter–anything that's being done excessively is a hike.

I know now that if you know God, then you'll have a better chance. I learned that His way was the only way, and how I did regret all those years being out and away from the Lord and thinking that I was the stuff. Come to find out I had been wasting my precious time and everyone else's time who was around me and loved me. The miracle is that I lived to tell the story. Maybe you will come to a point in life when no one wants to listen or maybe you're talking too fast, but I learned to tell folks the right thing and hopefully they are listening because all the churches I been to, and all the schools I attended, along with all the prayers, worked for me and it can for you.

Most people call it rock bottom but no, rock bottom is the grave. I just hit the bottom. And my higher power saved me. It's now something to think about, cause every time I went somewhere, folks were always talking to me about church. I raised three kids while on drugs and alcohol. And looking back now I still don't see how I made it through alive. There was a whole lot of praying and faith is what I call it, and it starts in the mind and you have to gain control of your mind, your body and with wisdom along with the Holy Spirit. I pray now for totally different things and I wish I had the knowledge then that I have now because I would never have ended up this way with two baby daddies. This is what I ended up with and both were drug dealers. I had a daughter by the first one and he was a whore and we didn't stay together too long because he went to jail for a three to six year stretch and by the time he got out I was gone and looking for someone better.

I used to gamble at the crap joints with my sisters, and the folks around town didn't know we had brothers, because they never hung out. There I met my sugar daddy and he kept my daughter and me well groomed with plenty of money in my pocket to buy drugs and anything else. After four years I got tired of him and was out looking for something else. He couldn't have kids and my daughter was turning five and I wanted another child. I never wanted marriage because I wanted to be my own boss, and I always went to school every day and went to church mostly every Sunday. I started running the streets and that was where I found my other baby's dad and he was a drug dealer slash alcoholic. And I had two kids by him and we fought all the time and I started stealing from him and everyone else, because he ran the streets and sold his drugs and did his thing, but he was never a good father and I was so high that I thought I was doing everything right, so I started taking his drugs because all he wanted to do when he came home was to eat dinner, have sex, and go to sleep.

He never washed a dish or took out the garbage or helped the kids with their homework.

This was when I got sick and tired so one day he came in and put my company out and we started fighting and as soon as he went to sleep, I stole his money and he didn't have any drugs on him. My eyes were wide and I took his money and ran to my brother and his wife and kids and when he found me, we would fight and I got tired of that too.

Now I was thinking of another way to get money because I never wanted to be the person that I saw in my friends doing so I would go shoplifting in them stores. I would get what I wanted for the kids, the other drug dealers and something for me and I usually got away with it. But the times I'd got caught were the times that I was a drug femur and in a desperate state. I went wild and was willingly doing anything for drugs and completely out of my mind and didn't give a care about nothing but my kids and my fix. I did put my drug habit over my kids most of the time.

I think now that when I got caught for stealing in my wrongdoings, this was when the Lord said that He'd had enough of my wrongs and he shut me down for a rest period and gave me a little time to think. That only helped me for a short period of time and I still went in and out of jail like a revolving door. With all my shenanigans, I was with the man on and off for over twenty years. As my kids got older they didn't like me as much and they definitely didn't like him. My younger daughter didn't care for men because her dad never showed her love or how to love.

I was the mom and dad and I was trying to do the best I could while staying high every day. I felt like I was doing good because one year my kids gave me a Mother's Day present on Mother's Day and a Father's Day present on Father's Day. That made me proud of myself.

I prayed when I went to church and I'd resort to prayer when I got in trouble. The kids started acting up in school and on the streets. I believe if you don't do time for your own crimes, that your kids will do the time later for you. My son became the gunslinger and both of my daughters became drug dealers. I'm just grateful that none of them became addicted. I know two of my kids did time for the both of us. The judge told me one day, if he saw me again in his courtroom that he would send me somewhere for a very long time and that slowed me down. Then their dad only went to the tank two or three times and he was the biggest criminal but his parents had money. You have to learn from your mistakes but I was so far gone I thought I was the stuff. I thought I was taking care of my kids, and my high, and the house, but little did I know that I was nothing. I just kept going in and out of jail and was mandated to a rehabilitation center and couldn't complete that either. My oldest daughter became a street walker and she was looking for love in all the wrong places and my other two became criminals. This went on for over thirty years. And my mom always told me to stop using before she died and it took her death and a whole lot of praying before I *really* heard her.

Choices are very important to any and everyone. A wise man once told me that if you can't grow plants, then how you going to raise kids? I figured it out and now I'm waiting to use it on my grand-kids. I did a truckload of praying for my kids because I didn't know how to be a sober parent. I learned that if we deceive ourselves and we think we can sow to the flesh without reaping corruption, sow the wind without reaping the whirlwind, then we cannot survive. I needed the Lord desperately. The world is prejudiced and it has been this way for many years. This means that I don't really know who rep-resents my best interest and who does not. This doesn't mean cream or color, this means knowing and knowledge. You must have the right kind of people in your life to grow for a better future. You need all kinds of help from different parties to make the world reach peace and harmony.

The Fool

IT'S A STORY that goes like this!!! Once upon a time, there was a King who delighted in his subjects. But of all the people, he liked his court jester the best. Whenever the King had too many problems. His court jester could always make him laugh. One day the King had a great idea. He had the court jester called to his chamber, The King was holding a little golden wand which He gave to the jester and said, 'My friend, when you find a bigger fool than yourself. You must give him this golden wand.' So the jester went out looking for a bigger fool than himself. He went through every village asking questions of one and all. His Royal Highness became sick and was dying. The court jester was called back to the palace. 'Hello, my little friend. I am going on a long, long journey from which I stall never return.' He was speaking of his death. The jester asked him, 'Are you prepared for that journey, your highness, and the King said NO... I haven't." 'Then I must present this golden wand to you.'

At last the jester had found a greater fool than himself. What about you? Have you prepared for your coming journey? If not, then you're in trouble, just like the King. A fool will reject knowledge, but a wise person will listen. I'm not going to say never, but I will take the n off and say ever, because there's a big difference in those words. For example, I will *never* do drugs again or *ever* do drugs again have a totally different meaning, but I don't know my future so I will say I ever don't want drugs in my life again. And back to what I said: A fool will reject knowledge, but a wise man will listen. O what a tangled web we weave when we first practice to deceive (by stealing robbing murdering--all crimes), and when we get caught we go to jail.

My kids' father is a living legend of recovery from a three month coma as a result of alcoholism. The Lord saw fit to allow him to recover and I think the Lord did it for me and others. He was very abusive and was a drunk. We fought all the time and if he was a good man then he would've helped me to be a good woman and I stayed and I prayed, but I can share the story to help others.

Forgiveness is when you don't forgive a person and they take the power over you, so you have to forgive them and then forgive yourself. God has the power to show you who He is. The same people you meet moving up you will meet coming down, but family is the worst of all. You thought you was doing the utmost for them while being an addict and once you got sober then that's another rehab situation. Every time you're with them and they bring up the past–anything you did wrong will make you feel some kind of way. It's affected by the remembrance of your past childhood and your drug addiction and you're stuck still trying to figure out how to move on. You must pay attention every day and pray that you will learn something new and how to do better.

Sin is anything that's indecent or immoral and will always take you further than you want to go, and keep you longer than you want to stay, and cost you more than you want to pay. But when we sow to the Spirit, we shall reap life. We shall reap what we sow in life. May we cease to sow the seeds of sin. Ouch! Something is in my eye.

My mom was raped and so was I. She never talked about it until I went through the same thing and it was like Silence of the Lamb and we all went to bed and woke up like nothing happened. I walked around with a chip on my shoulder for a long time and maybe still wear it now and then. I don't know if it shows or not but I know it's something of me that I cannot explain. This was one of the reasons I started using drugs, and I know that I betrayed my auntie and brought shame to my family. I asked her for forgiveness and the Lord too. I knew things would not be the same again, but how did I get to that point. It took a prison sentence for my cousin before the family actually started talking—and unburying the ugly past. I been messed up ever since cousin played with me in a sexual manner and then I was raped by the painter and no one acknowledged that. I've been very lost and all the lies and rape have a wretched affect on a person's life, especially when there is no counseling.

Now as far as Jesus Christ our Lord is concerned, he is my rock and that's how I was raised, but my mom slipped a little and so did I. Her slipping made me slip a lot more. Just sayin.' However, I don't fault her because now she is my rock too. My God gave me a second chance. I'm still learning every day how to move on and beyond with my God and my God only, because the Spirit is real and my parents are dead--both sets are gone to glory. The Spirit of my parents comes and goes from time to time and I know they are in heaven looking down on me. When they come to the surface all I do is smile because I know that they are in my presence and I thank God every day I wake up and every night I go to sleep, because God is my everything.

As I have lived I've learned that how you went about hurting people and yourself is how you fall down; and you often have to fall down in order to reach back up the righteous way to the top. You have to go through something to come around to something else. This means once you get sober, everyone is not going to love you back right away, except those who know the Lord and the ones who forgave you before you did the crime and ones who love you no matter what, and the ones who have forgiven you a long time ago, and those were the ones who prayed every day for you.

For example, if you started out on cigarettes and alcohol and moved up to something greater, and now you're ready to quit them all, you probably have to stop the most recent drug addiction and go backwards from the start unless you go cold turkey and that always seemed too hard if I wasn't locked down. Just thinking of being sober was a thought that went through my head from time to time, but when my mom passed, my third eye opened up wide and I started seeing better and thinking about what my mom said to me when she was living and that was to get off of drugs before they ripped me out of this world. I confessed to her while she was living. Not knowing if I was going to die any minute was a big step to take, so one day we all were cooking for a big family gathering as we always did and my favorite sister-in-law was there, and wouldn't say anything when she saw me every day and went to church mostly every Sunday. I started running the streets and that was where I found my other babies' dad and he was a drug dealer slash alcoholic, and my two sisters would start picking at me and I had a flashback from where the heck they were before I got to this point.

I told my mom that I was using drugs, and if anything ever happened to me or if somebody told her about me being on drugs that she wouldn't be in shock. After that day I started thinking about being sober and that thought stayed in my head more than usual, and every day after my mom passed I couldn't stop thinking about what she said but sad to say it took her passing before I could hear them clearly.

Far as being high, the thought would pass through my mind maybe once in a while and I was learning how not to react to thoughts and I learned that once a thought enters your mind then it must reach your heart to really start feeling it. It starts in the mind first so if I could just get it out of my mind then I could win this. I began feeling it was a mind game to not use and I live this every day.

I also heard about my past "get high buddies" and most of them are dead and a few are sober like me, and the ones that I'm not trying to seek I pray for them always. Some people cry about different things that others may pray about and we all need prayer because this is what makes the world a better place. I pray for world peace every day and I believe that prayer works. Family is all you've got and once you learn that then try to never disappoint them and you can't ever choose your family because it's already in the making, but you need to learn how to teach, preach, and pray for them. Even if they are good or bad, right or wrong they will always be your family.

My mom told me before she died that I'd been stuck in the pattern of repeating my past mistakes. If so, then how could I break this pattern to bring positive changes in my life? My desire is to be at peace within myself and with everyone around me. I know it's only God himself who can help me achieve this. I learned how to pray more and am still learning how to talk to God because He is my provider today, tomorrow, and always.

If you know the Lord, you will not fall into the hands of the devil. Human beings cannot completely trust in humans. We have to trust in the Lord and not humans because of their inability to remain consistently faithful. They will let you down over and over again, but God will not. The Lord never changes on you--you will leave Him but He'll never leave you or forsake you. I can have an unforgiving spirit toward someone who has wronged me or you think has wronged you. Can you hinder your own prayers? It is better to go and be reconciled with that person in Christ, and pray later rather than praying to God while bitterness is brewing inside of yourself. All parents have big expectations for their child. Once you have more than one child you believe your job should be easier, but instead it gets harder. The sixth child out of eight, I know my parents got tired. I have two older sisters and I had five brothers and two brothers were younger than me but it's hard on a parent and must be easier with two parents. After I was grown in age but not in mind, I started having bad relationships with men and being on drugs didn't help me one bit. How do you overcome an addiction after you stop using? How can you understand your family sober when you've been high for decades? How can you relate to your family and kids after you get sober? What happened in your childhood that led you to this point? "You know that God has never left you and now you found Him again for the second time. How did you get to this point? What happens next after you have learned the truth? Family is waiting on you.Once you beat that habit it's so easy to pick up another.

The bottom line of everything is to surrender to your higher power, in order to kick any and every addiction. You might think that you can do it by yourself but you cannot and if you have dreams just go for it, and make sure you have the right people around to support you. I am a soldier of the Lord, an angel. Rehab is the first step, and it's like going to church and joining, cause it seems like I have to do it for the rest of my life. It's like turning your whole life over to live a little longer and a lot greater. You have to do the footwork--you and the Lord. Family members and friends are cool with helping you, but the friends that loved me sober or high were the friends that are forever and once you get sober some are still hard to find. Once you learn how to stay sober, then you can find out how many friends you really have. I found out that I could count them on half of one hand, meaning very few.

I'm looking for new sober friends and happiness within myself. My mom passed a few years ago and I was caretaker for her until she died. I moved in with her because that was the thing to do. My siblings thought that it would be best, though they knew I was heavy on drugs. But I was the baby girl and didn't really have anything to do every day except stay high and not be broke. I had an income and was not happy with it. I was still trying to stay high. Then one day my mom repeatedly said to me, "I pray you get off of them drugs before I leave this world," but she never said die. All she ever asked of me was to stop using. I know that God gives signs and he sends people your way and if you are blind and cannot see then you won't see them coming or going.

First she was sick just a little bit and would talk all the time about getting well and going shopping and to church and the bingo hall, and she wasn't getting better as the days went by. She felt better she would talk about going shopping and getting better and that never happened. Once she passed I lost all the desire for drugs, but I was still living with a drug addiction and had an ex-dealer and ex-alcoholic on the side. He came out of the coma and started loving me the way he should have done before he got sick, but by that time I had lost all the love I had for him because it was strange that I still loved him but I wasn't in love and he still was my kids' father. When my mom passed, I had warrants up my tail, and I used to use my sister's name every time I got caught. One day she came over to my house, (mommy's favorite) and said, "Stop using my name because you don't know what I'm doing and I may be Mommy's favorite but I may not, and the next time you use my name I'm going to go to the police station and tell them myself that you have been using my name and I'll have them pick you up for perjury."

I got scared and after that day I never used her name again. Mom passed and she was a shopaholic and had so much stuff. But she also loved people and was willing to help any and everyone. Of course, she also loved to shop and play bingo too. It seemed like she would go shopping and see something on sale and hold it up and say, "Yeah, I know so-and-so. She can fit into this." She would buy it, and she had a ton of stuff. My mom loved to look good and she could dress to impress. I used to go through her closet looking for something to wear to church with her and she had a lot to choose from.

I knew that she was real sick when the church started coming to her. That was sad to watch her die slowly and when she passed her last breath, I didn't want to see that last one because every day it looked like she was taking her last. I watched her suffer and I heard her cry and I know that she was preparing herself for the Lord. My sisters and I went through the closet looking for something to wear and we found out that she left all her clothes to my oldest sister, who was too small and my niece who was too young for my mom's clothes. They both didn't want anything; my niece said it was out of style. I was glad because I'd been rocking mostly all of my mom's clothes, shoes and this one hat. It was the hat I wore to the funeral and my auntie wanted it. I believe that the only reason she wanted the hat was because it looked good on me and everybody said it did and she was still hating on her husband from back before as being a manipulator and a man who's for drugs and whatever. I believe that her husband pumped up the painter for the painter to rape me and then he was still wondering how or when he could make his move on me and I was naïve to the fact.

I fell along the way but I'm better now and my mom is gone. I know my mom understands now and she knows that this is a good thing because she is happier gone than being here with the stress, pain and agony that probably led to her sickness and death. Several of my aunts came to get clothes and stuff and I had the first pick of everything. But one aunt that lived next door would help my mom when I went out for air, and this one hat was so pretty. I wore it to the funeral and my other aunts, friends, and my siblings said I looked good in the hat. Now my auntie from next door wanted that hat too, and out of all the goods, clothes, and other things that my mom had, she only wanted that hat--the one I was wearing. Then I caught her sneaking tapes when she thought I wasn't looking. She claimed that she didn't want nothing, but she was getting things behind my back. This wasn't a problem but the problem was that she said she didn't want nothing but that hat I wore. I didn't have nowhere to go and no place to put stuff but I wanted my mother's hat. After the funeral she told my other aunts and my siblings about this and she said all she wanted was that hat and she started something that day but I thought I'd finish it. I finally decided to turn myself in at the county jail where I had been running from a warrant–a warrant that I was tired of running from. And all I was thinking about is that everyone said I looked so good in that hat and I wanted to keep it, because it was my mom's. That was a terrible idea.

Now mom is gone to heaven and left me alone to think about all that was said. I woke up one morning less than one month after she passed and got on the train and went to turn myself in and the justification in my mind was "I'm tired of running."

When I got there I had two warrants in two different counties so I had around $600 in my pocket, thinking that I would be able to make bail, but no it was $1500 to walk out of one jail and I got shipped to another. Didn't know what they wanted with me, I was just thinking about why both counties were after me and exactly what I had done. Both counties just wanted money and I didn't have enough. This was one of the saddest days of my life.

I woke up one morning and realized that my oldest child hated me and my other two were in jail too. I was embarrassed to look in the mirror and I didn't. What I learned right then and there was if you don't stand up for something then you'll fall for anything. I learned that you are in control of your destiny. I learned that you sometimes have to go backward to move forward. This was my meaning in order to be whole.

You have to review everything you've been through. As a kid you have to go back in your mind to remember what all have you've faced and all you've seen as far as money, people, strangers and friends have to recollect in your mind and you have to pass through it again, and once you identify such a place and begin to use it regularly then a kind of aura surrounds it. Your prayer room can become a holy place –a place where you meet with God and if you don't know how to pray and want to learn then ask God that too. Just find yourself a quiet place free of distractions. Ask for His presence and His kindness and just start babbling, pouring your heart out and another kind of meaningless repetition is often heard at dinnertime. A nutritional nightmare. God's will might be for the person to say AMEN, push back from the table and type up a theology class dissertation. Or it might simply be the realization that you must love the Lord your God with all your heart, all your soul, and all your mind. This is the first and greatest commandment.

After I got sentenced for a year, I was praying to go home. I was so upset and I knew that I had to make a decision to do right. I had lost my friends. My kids' father always tried to help but he was to sick. I wanted to go to my home that I didn't have anymore. I felt so bad that all I could do was drop to my knees and pray and I did. But then I became silent and didn't want to communicate with anyone and didn't want to talk to my family or my jail mates. I was a walking zombie for several weeks.

I started wondering about what would happen to my kids if something bad ever happened to me. I started sobering up real fast in my mind and I started going to church and seeing a counselor for help because I really needed it more now than ever. The church folks and the counselors helped me get back on track and I came to a stark realization. My kids were away in jail all except one and she wasn't loving me at all. I started reminiscing about my past and my lifestyle on drugs and how much I had hurt people and how many people's lives I messed up. All I could hear was my mom's words and looking back at my kids while I was high and thinking that they didn't know, but they did. Then came

the memories of living with my mom to help her while she was sick and dying. I thank God for that and it lasted one year of being with her until she passed away. All I could think of was what she used to say to me and that was "I hope you get off them drugs before I die or just get off that stuff before I leave this world." I tried so hard and I prayed so much, but the devil would always overpower me. I thought my prayers weren't real and I felt like I was just doing something because this was the thing to do but little did I know, He was listening and I learned later how to stop using drugs. Another thing I learned was don't put pressure on just one person to do any and everything for you. Just have a number of choices and keep a close relationship with them all.

While I was locked down, every night when I went to sleep my mom would wake me up and appear in my vision with a smile and a soft calm gentle voice saying, "Give auntie that hat back because that was the only thing she wanted."

I sat up and was thinking that it was just a dream but I could hear her voice and see her face so clearly and I tried to ignore it several times. Every night it became more powerful and clearer. Finally, I opened up my eyes to listen and she said in a nice pleasant voice, "Give that hat to auntie," and I tried to ignore it again and again but each night was the same as the last. Before the week was out it became a problem. She was messing with my sleep, so one night I finally answered her and said, "Okay Mom, I will when I get out of here."

Every night after that I slept like a champ. Knowing that I was locked up, I'd realized that I could still be with my mom in spirit but once I answered her she left me alone. She had peace and I did too. The very next day I wrote this letter to my auntie and here's how it went.

Hi Auntie

How are you doing ? My mother has been talking to me in my dreams every night and I asked one of my jail mates what does that mean?

And she said tell her good night so I did and the next night she came again and I told my jailmate it's something else and I think she's trying to tell me something. I waited until the next night and my mom appeared again and said 'give auntie that hat because that's all she said she wanted from me,' and I could hear her as if she was lying next to me. I started thinking about you and knowing that you lived next door to my mom and was there with her and for her when I was out and about. As soon as I get out I'm going to bring you the hat. By the way, I caught the train here to turn myself into the law enforcement and I had warrants and was tired of running. Auntie, I stopped using drugs and I went to rehab to learn how to get sober. Then I I went and turned myself in at the jail, and as soon as I get out of here I will bring you that hat.

And I signed it like she would feel my pain.

After the system released me, I was paroled to a shelter in Chicago, the city where I was born. That was where the Bible program came into play. I joined the Bible program to learn about God and to stay away from old friends and places. I still remembered that I'd said to myself that I never liked Chicago and didn't ever want to live there again based on my past experience of going to work with my mom as a little girl and watching the news every day on television.

The Lord can change your mind from ever to never. And I had to go back there because of my behavior in my past. Once my mom remarried, I was so glad when she told us that we were moving to the suburbs, and she took us out of the city and moved us to a small town where everyone knew everybody else and now as I got older I started thinking about myself and wondering if that was a good decision. But later I found out that it was a good decision to raise kids with discipline.

Back to the shelter after I got out of prison, there was this little elderly lady that caught my eye and I couldn't help but watch her. She always would ask me, "Would you like to join the Bible program, sweetie?" I was running backward and forward to the suburbs looking for a place and making sure to see my parole board officer at the shelter but never wanted to live there. I finally found me a place within a couple of months and when I unpacked my things I then found that hat. I took out like a bat out of hell and I ran over the train tracks like a car to the next town where auntie lived and rang the doorbell. She answered, and I handed her the hat box in her hands and said, "My mama told me to give you this hat" and I walked away. There was no problem then and I had plenty of peace thereafter. Don't sweat the small stuff.

The Holy Spirit and families' spirit are real and I am here to say there is a God, He's got me through everything and he'll do the same for you. Now I'm good as better and better is blessed. Praying helps, so please don't ever think that it doesn't, and the Holy Spirit is real too. My mom's hat let me know right away about the Holy Spirit.

With Christ risen and your higher power, a child may stray away but not for long. The final destiny is not the picture of heaven that you have stuck in your head. You know the image of pearly gates and streets of gold. Instead it's of the universe, so it would look a lot like here. The pearly gates streets of gold stuff, that's a picture of me and Jesus, my spiritual bridegroom. It is a picture of me as a bride and in church. The gate of heaven is a great pearl, the only precious stone made by pain, suffering and finally death. It's all about relationships and a simple shared life.

I settled into my new place but it wasn't right. I started falling back into my old habits and ways and the signs were very clear because my new friend was using and my apartment actually acted like it was high too. Everything in the apartment started falling apart, and every month when it was time to pay rent it felt like I was moving in again because stuff would break and stuff needed fixing. And all I could envision and think about was the little old elderly lady from the shelter and how she used to invite me to the Bible program and I never answered. She used to walk around in my head and then whenever I thought about her, it seemed my place was becoming more and more fragile. Things would break and the roof started leaking from one room to another, then the furnace wouldn't work, and the floors started peeling. For real, it went from one thing to another.

One day the landlord said, "I don't want you to sue me so here's seven hundred and fifty bucks because this is what I would have to pay if I evict you and try to put you out so this is for you to move out and find you another place." He said, "I know this building is old and I don't want you to sue me.

I could have sued him, but I took the money, put my stuff in storage and went to see what that little old lady was talking about. I also began to run from that new guy and his drugs. I took a second look at my life and I said, "My daughter is in jail and my son just went back to jail. And I am still straddling that fence of addiction..." . I woke up one morning and the walls started talking. I could hear clearly and I ran to freedom. —I raced to God's house to learn how to live a different way, and to have a relationship with God--I mean a real one. And I wanted to learn everything that I could about Him and to have a relationship with my kids. . My parole was over and I needed something real.

Now I was really there and this was the best thing that ever happened to me, They had GED classes, they had clothes, Bible study classes, beds, and food. The breakfast food was ok but other meals sucked. The Saturday dinners were delicious. Every Saturday was the day we had to dress up for radio station and I loved Saturdays, and we also had to dress up on Sundays too. But Sunday food tasted like lunch and dinner on the other days.

I learned a lot. They took us to visit other places and we sang songs and some of us stood up and talked about our deliverance and experience from our past. I wanted to stand up every time they would ask. One day I asked the Lord to help me because I wanted this so bad but I was nervous and my heart started racing and my mind wouldn't stand still. I raised my hand and stood up and started giving my testimony. And it went like this, "I was born a sinner and my past has been all bad. I was raised as a spoiled brat, and didn't ever need or want for anything. I thought I had it all. I got caught up in the fast lane with drugs, beauty, and glamour. I decided I didn't need God's way and I could be my own boss. Later I lost my self-respect my kids' respect and the respect of my family. I went to jail and I lost my kids to the prison walls along with myself.

"When my mom passed both of my kids were in prison. Before she passed, she prayed that I would get off of drugs before she went. I tried but it would only last a few days, or I'd get locked up, or get pregnant. I have smoked up mansions, duplexes, town-houses, and limousines. I learned that all money isn't good money, because I didn't know what to do with it when I had it. I would still go in them stores and steal any and everything I wanted. Then I would take the money to the dope man and after all of that my kids would suffer and they didn't have no good direction. All the druggies and everyone else would say I was doing a good job with my kids and that blew my head up. I really thought I was the stuff, but I learned that they said that because my kids weren't in the system. Later on in life two of my kids went to prison while I was in there too. I felt like I didn't have nothing left to live for. And I knew that I had to do this for me first in order to do something for them. God pulled me out in his timing and not mine."

This was my testimony and I started praying and praying for my kids and myself. I wanted to show them who their parent really is. I didn't want no more nicknames from back on the block--the drug block of insanity, hatred, and disrespect. I learned that God is good all the time and He will never leave you or forsake you. I was supposed to be there for a year, but I only stayed seven months. After seven months the devil began working on my hormones and I started liking some guy and when he left the mission, I left behind him and that was another bad mistake. It only lasted for a couple years on and off. I found a church and a school everywhere I went and started attending. I asked him to go with me and he said that he was a witness and he started taking the studies and the witness. People would come by and he would say that I couldn't be there doing that time because we wasn't married. I was so lost and desperate that I was ready to change my religion. I stayed in church wherever I landed but I told him to go and serve his God and I said there are many religions but I learned to serve one God. And I never went back because I knew I was doing too much.

I left and went to another state and finished school and got my GED. My kids started coming around me, but we all were scattered though trying to communicate regularly. First my oldest daughter moved from Nevada to be with me and the next year my younger daughter came. My son came to visit and said he wouldn't live there so we all moved together to a new state trying to get to know each other and a new place. I learned to bounce back wherever I was at and I did. I started school again, found a church again, and housing. I was tired of trying to make new friends. I didn't want any new friends; I wanted my old friends and I wanted them to be like me, sober, but I knew that wasn't going to happen. I was sad on the inside for a while and just looked happy on the outside. I was missing my old friends at the same time I was trying to find a new life for my kids. I didn't know how to live sober and it was scary. I lived happy with my kids but my past will never leave my mind.

The world always blared out some breaking news for us to panic about. It's sad to know that this new virus is eighty percent deadly and it doesn't matter if you are rich, poor, or loved. It doesn't matter if you were born healthy and been living a healthy life or if you was born unhealthy. Corona or COVID-19 doesn't care. It's possible these new diseases will keep continually popping up. These are some of the ones we're familiar with like cancer, unintentional injuries, chronic low respiratory diseases, and cerebrovascular diseases, Alzheimer's disease, influenza, pneumonia, strokes and diabetes. This disease is deadly, not visible like some of the other ones we know about and it's in the air. You can't see it and it's silent and deadly.

The Bible tells us not to be afraid because He is coming for you. You won't miss it; you'll receive what God says and HE makes no mistakes, so my theory is: stop being discombobulated about something you can't control: listen, pray, teach, and keep following the rules of the road. You can't go wrong with this COVID-19. The devil stays busy and we need to learn how to pray, how to get along with each other, and help others if you can and have a jump start step ahead of the enemy. My theory is that this is another way to get rid of some of us. There's so many people everywhere you go, and everything is in the fast lane and no one takes it slow anymore, but God knows what HE is doing.

The government knows how to stand us up and how to sit us down and I don't trust them. I believe they are manipulative and will cross any and everyone to stay ahead and beyond before it's over. I believe that in the eighties was when more and more drugs were smuggled into the U.S. and out into the communities. They messed up folks with crack and other drugs to harm the black communities and others. This was serious nationwide crime. I was a victim and my kids were too. Being in the streets back in the eighties was about drugs, and no knowledge and no one to help. Then everyone was doing it and the neighbors went bad. I could be wrong, but my theory is that the population has grown overwhelmed by crime and the anarchists want some of us to be gone and this is their route. From Corona to killings is just another step so that we cannot figure it out.

We have no control. If we don't stop, think, and listen, we are sitting ducks. We need to pray and think about how we got to this point. We've been staying home until they figure this out. The parents are on drugs and who's doing the babysitting? Kids are raising themselves with no direction. The government knows what they are doing but if we can recognize the facts and come together to man up for this pandemic, maybe we can learn how not to do the wrong things that are tempting us in this world today. It seems like the devil is running this and the government is still governing. People are making bad choices all over the planet. I have learned from experience and I know that I can't control what's going on, but I will pray and ask if there's a solution that we need to know. Then I wish someone would share. I don't think everybody honors God and some people don't know Him or care about righteousness. Me, I want to help folks without harming them or myself. If I can, there's no problem. I stay out of harm's way.

Everyone is not on the same page and the world doesn't owe anyone nothing but we all need a hero from time to time. I'm just wondering how to be that hero. Our higher power has us and we need to keep the faith. The good book says there will be a coming of the Lord someday so I put it in the Lord's hands because God knows and He is always in control. Just seek him.

I know if we are not killing each other fast enough or dying quickly enough from the drugs then Satan, the great destroyer, will find another way to kill off some of us but this is only my theory. I know that things happen and they happen for reasons we may never understand or learn why. But most of us are still lost and some will never be helped. God does things sometimes to get everyone's attention. The ones who are not listening will pass away.

Back in 1929 times were hard and folks were poor and they called it the Depression and while that was going on my parents were about to be born. I used to hear my mom talk of it and she said one Christmas she only got a pair of shoes and an apple. It must have been hard on her and my grandparents. I also heard her say that folks starved to death and she said she will never be poor again. When she died she was rich in heart and in love and it was not about money though she had that too. My perspective is that you should not sugar coat the past because the past is what makes a greater future. My prayer is to be humble and listen, because I know that some folks in the world are prejudiced. The brothers in our towns carry guns and we can be killed at a stoplight and they have been killing one another for years so how can we stop this madness?

Now some folks think it is the end of world, or is it something we must go through because we are not listening to the Lord? Meaning stop the killings, the crimes, the drugs, and the disrespect. Go seek and listen to your higher power and live by the good book. It seems like every so many years passes by and here comes another depression from buying everything off the shelves like in 2000, there were flashlights, water, panic, and they said the world was coming to an end on the following day. This seems more scary now than it was back in 1929, hard times of depression but this time, it's a deadly weapon. The only thing that is different is that we are not as poor as our parents were back then, but it's all on the same page–just a different date, time and situation. It's all still controlling the universe and killing some of us off again. I also think that the population has grown and kids are having babies out of wedlock. We stop dating and learning about a person then marriage and only having one baby daddy and one baby mom, and take blood tests before birth because when the baby grows up it will be good to know if the two of you are the true father and mother.. What happened to the good old days? The good old days were much funnier and understandable, how can we find as much fun as our parents had if we don't do the right things by listening to our parents' advice, even if their advice isn't always what we want to hear! Why have we stopped praying and listening to the words of the truly wise? We should place ourselves under God's hand and His control. If we did we would not have to go through this crap. And everyone would be happy and healthy and I believe that you have to do this on earth because this is your first heaven or hell.

We need to do as they say and we need to pray and seek Jesus Christ and have faith because I pray all the time. O Lord, we need to pray for ourselves and others because sometimes folks get careless and comfortable with the way things are and other folks never stop and think about how to make it better. Some just don't know how to grow or never thought about it or they could care less. Life is meaningless to them. They're stuck in their own ways and happy with it and not looking for a change until something catastrophic happens. The sickness has aroused folks' intolerance. They are realizing that they forgot how to live healthy and happy by playing these mind games. Folks should already know what's going on. The Corona virus is telling folks to get closer to their kids and family members and take time to listen to your kids and teach them something because they are the next generation. The population is over-populated and Corona is killing so many people because the world is too full of folks and no one is listening to God. Now if you know better then you should do better and shouldn't have a problem with this matter. If you're on drugs or drinking your life away you will never understand what the heck is going on. Every morning you wake up and wonder how to survive the Corona, and all schools are closed for this virus.

I see now this is the time to pray and time to spend with your kids and to teach them how to become better adults. Learn to listen to your child closer and you will learn something new every day. This should be better than going to work in your mind because this is not your nine to five. This is your everyday 24/7 job, time to be with your kids. It should feel better and don't forget that this is your number one job.

Are you asking God why? We should be asking when but we all know that the people of earth continually do what they think is best for them. As far as the government and the president are concerned, we don't have control and what we need to realize is there is a higher power bigger than the government and the president and it is the God of the universe. If we continue to do as we please and not as God pleases for us then we still have a lot to learn. Now I'm learning how to save money and how to pray, and stay out of harm's way, because we all are born sinners, sinners from the womb.

We should never stop praying and teaching, reading and listening to the good book. God has this and if he agrees then I do too. You know the Bible says that our days are numbered and we doesn't know how it will end. Our bodies are ephemeral. Teach me to see beyond the mortal, beyond the ephemeral and, instead, at my Lord. Plunge my insight deep into your words.

Now that you know the knowledge of loving one another, if you don't like your own company, then who else will? The knowledge of the good book and how to live happily on this earth is to learn how to be and do better within yourself. Once you understand that then it's no problem to live on earth happily and face eternity with peace and joy. God has this and will do whatever needs to be done to get our faith and attention. Now if you don't understand why, then you are left out of God's plan. Is this the devil or is this God? If you know Him there's no question about what has happened, because He's got the whole world in His hands,, and He is in control as far as making this world a better place in spite of all the crime, hatred and violence. The world has fallen from what is good to what seems so bad. I know that as long as you're loving God and living for Him that God has your back through thick and thin. He will always be there for you.

Now our higher power is taking over because most of us don't believe in Him and some of us don't seem to recognize Him as our higher power. We pretend to listen and sometimes we pay attention. Folks, everyone needs to pay attention to what God has put you on this earth for and how He has kept you here for His ultimate reasons.

Young, old, and babies, God will do what He has to do for His mission. God is always in control and we should learn His way, because His way is the only way. We won't know our check-out date, but we know our birthday. God has this and He has the whole world thinking, and if this is what it took, so be it. Always remember that He is in control and help those with knowledge and help those without knowledge. Help the ones who don't listen and don't know, and if you cannot help those people then just help yourself, your family and the other listeners. Now, remember, if you don't listen and pray then you don't have the key of life. Stay away from wrongdoers, pray and hang around positive energy folks.

My desire is to be at peace with myself and everyone in my life. Only God knows and can help those to achieve their goals. God is my provider today, tomorrow, and always. If you have the Lord deep in your heart, mind and soul, you will not fall into the hands of man. I understood this now, at a later age. I'm sad because now my third eye is opened up wide to see what I've been doing to myself and my family and to let me know that it's never too late to start over. I used to spend every dime I got, but now I save every dime I get. I never finished the rehab programs; I just went to sober up for a moment but I don't use drugs anymore. I still need counseling because of my past including my childhood. I need to learn how to live with myself and how to talk to my kids and family. I want to tell them something new every day that will help them become better persons.

God has did wonders with me and I know that he is not done with me yet. Mostly all my old get-high buddies are dead or appear dead. I have two left that are sober and they live in different states. I still talk to them from time to time. God has shown me that He saved me so I would see that there's a better way and he did that to my kids' father as a recovered alcoholic who lay in a coma for two and a half months. He came a long way from being sick and I know there was a lot of praying along the way. Your higher power has your back and you have to seek him, pray, and be righteous. Surrender your life to the Lord and talk the talk and walk the walk. Stop and listen for Him to respond to you, because if you don't stop, wait and listen, you won't hear His voice when He responds back to you. Listen to what you can learn from your surroundings and from your child. The whole world is not prejudiced but some still are. This is what I gathered when I learned how to do the right thing. I let life turn me upside down so I could learn to live right side up.

After going back and forward from Iowa to Minnesota, I learned patience while waiting on my kids to return home. And I liked Iowa better because it was a small town like where I grew up in and manageable as far as learning places and getting around. Minnesota was harder to find my way around, but I ended up in Minnesota because my sister used to treat me bad and she was very disrespectful to me. I was forced back to Minnesota and there I felt needed by my niece and she wanted me as much as I needed her, though little did she know it. I needed to be needed somewhere and her family made me feel like home.

I grew stronger while waiting for my own family to return home. Being there, she gave me hope and strength. This was something to look forward to while waiting on the return of my kids. I learned how to get back on the right track for myself and my kids. I attended school and church. I started taking her kids to church and to the library. My niece and her husband had their own friends and we used to play cards on the weekends and her husband's friends were mostly family and out of the four brothers I was a partner with one of them and we used to play cards together. One of them knew both of my sisters from back home and we became friends. My niece was very much younger than me and always dressed high- maintenance. I didn't want to have that kind of fun anymore. I just wanted my kids, and I wanted to show them who I really was, so I found my own place and moved back to Iowa. I sent for my card partner to live there with me and to save money because the rent in Minnesota is higher than the rent in Iowa. I thought he could get a better life, but he still drinks to this day. I left him behind and moved out of state after I got my GED. I gathered up my kids finally and moved to another state that was closer to home. I moved to Indiana and this is where I'm at now.

Once you get sober and off drugs, everything isn't okay. Now that you've been on and off of drugs for over 35 years, you are trying so hard to stay sober and it feels like something else is wrong, so you think back to before you started drugs. You think about what really matters and your mind is playing tricks in your head and all you want to do is to be sober again. I learned that one high is too many and a thousand was never enough.

I sing now. I sing because I'm happy and I sing because I'm free and I sing hallelujah and I rejoice in the Lord and I pray for the world every day. I remember back in the days of my addiction. At that time singing with joy was never on my mind. I'm so blessed and this is my miracle and my belief. God is good all the time and all the time God is good. Love can be bitter but it can also be sweet, so now I can think about things and I know who and what to love. Part of life is recognizing the future and praying for a better one. I have dreams and

I keep the faith, and trust God to lead me in a better direction. I was back and forth traveling from one state to another and one of those states my sister lived in and the other one my niece lived in. But my niece treated me better than my sister and my sister had been my best friend—at least that is what I thought.

My niece took me in as a babysitter and this was what she thought and little did she know that I needed her more than she needed me and more than can be measured. Now she's like a daughter to me and I can help her and I know she'll help me. Every time I go to visit her and the family, I look out for her kids and I put education on their minds and I do it in a joking way because I make them laugh. I know I made some bad choices and now because of my bad choices, I don't have any friends. I'm sober and looking for my new sober friends, and I keep praying and staying focused for a better future. I stay in my praying closet to study. I learned to stay away from folks to keep my sanity. I know that some folks still think that I'm getting high or in slavery to my mind and they keep treating folks wrong and saying awful things to others and to me. Nevertheless I can't say that I don't care what they think of me. I just don't want no trouble and they need to stay away. I finally got the mother and daughter relationship with my girls and I'm still working on some flaws. My son will take longer than my daughters, because he is the baby and we're still learning each other and I'm still working on my sobriety.

As years pass you by the faraway chances of who you want to be become extremely frustrated, so don't waste precious time on worthless things, or something that may be nothing farther up the road. You have to look for red flags and pay attention because we all can be born again Christians. The signs will tell you. Then you'll know right from wrong, and nobody or no one can tell you different. Find time to do better and learn something new every day. Plant yourself around positive energy people and learn how to grow with what you know, because your knowledge will help others in the future. A mind of destruction is time that's been wasted for an engagement of positivity and inner beauty. Learn, pay attention, and stay focused on what is righteous, and learn righteousness through all your heart and soul in the days to come. Learn how to live with yourself before living with anyone else. Learn your way and then ask yourself questions to see how it may sound before asking anyone else. Then you can learn their ways. Remember, the Lord is first, then your kids, and you are last.

This is how you can deal with other people.

It was so terrible when I went to prison and learned that two of my kids was in prison too. That was a big eye opener for me. I was devastated and learned later that this was probably the reason that I'm not a grandmother yet. I learned that every day you should improve your life even if it's bad or good, right or wrong, and I do learn something every day and I pray every day for a new day and I ask the Lord to keep me here to see some grand babies. I don't know what His plan is for me. But I will say that I'm waiting patiently. Jesus Christ is all I need to know and the Holy Spirit that lives in me is all I need to stay focused on. I love everyone but I'm afraid of the Spirit inside of them.

Praying, teaching, and guidance can make anybody a better human being. I talk to my higher power four to five times a day. I pray for what I didn't do and for what I should be doing. I'm lost but I keep moving on in the right directions. I keep prayers in my heart. I know that I will need rehabilitation for the rest of my life. I look forward every day to help someone's spirit and to keep finding my way differently from the way I used to be.

After all, I've made apologies numerous times. I'm trying to live in a better state of mind from where I was in my past. I'm so much older and I still have a lot to do. I don't have it all together now or ever, but I know I need counseling more than rehab and now that I rehab my physical ways, I need help on my thinking. The wind blows where it will, you hear the sound of it, but you don't know when it comes or whither it goes. It's the same with everyone else who is born of the Spirit. Except a man be born again, he cannot enter the kingdom of

Christ. What is born of the flesh is flesh, what is born of the Spirit is Spirit. A person must be born twice. And if you never give your heart, then you won't have to worry about it being broken. Keep God first in all you do. God bless us all; I always pray for world peace.

I remember my mom telling me that when she used to leave me on the bed with my sister and brother they were left there to watch me. But when she came back to get me I was behind the bed on the radiator. She couldn't believe I didn't cry. I just lay there until she found me. My sis and bro would run out of the room when my mom came back. My mom would exclaim, "Where's my baby?" and as soon as I heard her voice I would cry out. My sis and bro would get the belt, but my head had been bumped many times and the fears are still there.

Sometimes a person doesn't know why they have scary feelings and may never know what happened, and sometimes a parent may not realize that their child needs help. It may be a bump on the head, or not being watched closely. And even a child maybe abused or be the abuser at an early age. The parent or parents are not paying attention to them, or just not preaching, teaching, and adding lots of prayer. You may never know what your condition is but I know everyone has one because nobody is perfect and there's no perfect person on earth. Everyone is praying to go to heaven, and I believe that you have to live it down here on earth first before entering into the kingdom of heaven.

I believe that I need to attend a counseling session at least twice a week. Some folks call them shrinks but the best name for them is expensive but helpful. I need to go and see someone costly and get help. I need someone to let me spill my brain to and they help me with what's going on in my head. I need to do rehab again and work it until I'm better. I need God working to change my way of thinking and, after all that, I need to be loved and taught how to love again.

Now thinking back to my addiction, I started weed first, then alcohol and as I got older and met new people, I ended up on cocaine. I used to sell weed to my friends at school and I started selling cocaine.

But I became my biggest customer. I would take the money out of one pocket and put it in the other. I learned that you cannot win on this stuff, or being around it, because there's no win. Either way it's death or jail. I decided that I wanted more and I could not go out like this. I started thanking the Lord for being there when everything seems lost. I started thanking Him for the strength to face my problems, thanking Him for giving me a second chance to get things right for the mistakes I made, and most of all, thanking him for bringing everything together so I can build and move on. I asked God to take me down to the river and wash me clean in the water. It's time to bury the past

I think that the Corona virus has brought family closer together and kids can spend more time with their parents and the parents can spend more time with their child. I believe that COVID-19 is a stay-at-home airborne disease happening before the next generation is on deck and will take time out for them to help them grow. This is just my theory, and I don't know anything different.

I'm waiting on some grandkids so I can teach them, preach to them, and pray with them. I wanna show them and tell them how to save money and how to go for their dreams and to put some cash away for their future, calling it a rainy day and money for college so they can be anything their hearts desire. They must aim high and higher than their expectations because they can be anything they want to be. They just have to have the vision and put in the work to make it happen.

Remembering back to when we used to visit my aunts, I hated when we went to one of their houses, because auntie had a son that played different. He always liked the game called It or Tag. He played it very differently, and he used to catch me under the tent and fornicate with me in an unhealthy way. I didn't like that game no more after playing several times with him, but I never said anything because I didn't know how. He would chase us and feel on me when he caught me and to this day I wonder if he did my other sister like that or if he did his sisters like that. Another thing I was disappointed about was they had all the board games on the shelves and the shelves looked like we was in a harmless Toys R Us store but when he grew up, everything came out into the light, and we found out he had done the same thing to some of my nieces and some cousins too. He ended up in prison for rape. He went with a prostitute and didn't pay her for her service, then she cried rape and called the police on him and that was when everything began to hit the fan. The family started talking about it and it was sad. After he got out of prison, some family members still didn't like him, but I forgave him because that is the thing to do. If you don't forgive people who harm you then you'll carry it on your shoulders for the rest of your life and it could tear you down. That left part of my brain lost and disturbed. To this day I'm still lost and I know I need help. I really need someone to talk to and someone to listen. My mom's other sister was not as bad–at least that was what I thought. And my mom and her partied every weekend at one another's house. My rich auntie was loaded and would give us anything, but her husband was a whore and he messed around on her a lot and now thinking back about him, as I got older he had his eyes on me.

Once again when I got caught up on drugs, he played with my intelligence and I was weak when he assigned me drug missions. I started off being a runner for him. I did this or that and I was getting paid and it seemed fun at first until one day he had this gofer run to me. His maintenance guy came and gave me a big bank roll, hundreds of dollars and I fell for it. This was the second worst day of my life. Because the first one was when I started using drugs. I regret both times and I prayed for my forgiveness. With all the parents I had and all the siblings I had, there wasn't no teaching or preaching, but I know somebody somewhere was praying for me. I learned off the streets and hanging out with older folks. I believe I learned too many of the wrong things.

I would communicate with my mom but I couldn't with my dad. They lived in different cities and I was around my mom more than my dad. Guess I lived around my mom for over fifty years and with my dad only fifteen years. He died early from alcoholism and that became a problem in my addiction. He gave me everything but knowledge, and as he was getting sick he started talking about college and by that time, I was only listening to me. Now that I have been through and seen both sides of life, I know now that it can get better every day. I remember my mom telling me that everyone has a moment in life that they will have the choice to live a great life. Think of your happiness and the dreams you love, put your whole heart into it, and you can be successful. With that in mind, I kept that in my heart, along with the drug addiction, and nobody to talk to, or nobody to listen. I learned the hard way because after I came out of the shadows as a lost little girl, I did all the talking and I was a big help for most of my get-high friends. All of them came with problems. I thought that I was on top of the world by counseling them with their problems. I would say to myself that I have a PhD and I didn't have to go to school to get it. I felt famous or rich some days, and these were my crackhead so-called friends. They did have another place to go where they wouldn't have to put up with a lot of crap. I didn't need for anything but I didn't realize that my kids did. I really thought I had it together. No praying, or just praying for the moment, no teaching, and just teaching for the high, and no guidance counselor to direct me back on the right path.

The way to understand anyone else's life is to walk in their shoes. All those years being out and away from the Lord, I thought I was managing well but I was just a showcase of quiet laughs behind my back. I was wasting my time and everyone else's time who loved me and those who were around me. The miracle is that I lived to tell the story and I learned how to live on and better without drugs. All the churches and all the praying worked for me and it can for you. I'm not going to say never but I will take the N off and say ever. Because there's a big difference in those words. For example, I will never do drugs again, but I don't know my future, so I will say I don't ever want drugs around my life again. Drugs had me figured out and I thought I was grown. I thought I had the whole world figured out, but I learned that a fool will reject knowledge and a wise man will listen. I am done being a fool for drugs. Some know the Bible and some don't. I believe in the righteousness of the Lord and I learnt how to do the right things through Christ.

They keep saying that the world is going to end soon, but now with the Corona virus going on and people are catching it and getting sick, maybe dying. Who's to say what's really happening because they don't know. You need to give respect so you can receive. Learning and knowing about your higher power is a lesson to be learned. God knows and it's his-story and it's going to be always his story. This is what I get out of the word History because it's always someone's story. And we all should start today by teaching our kids and others with whom we come in contact how to pray and how to live heaven in your heart. Our kids are the future and the next generation. There is a God, there is a Spirit, and it is real. It's as real as our daily need to use the bathroom or eat meals and as real as learning how to tie your shoes so you don't trip or fall.

I found my miracle, my beliefs, and I'm not proud of how I came to this point because this was the long way around. If I had better teaching, preaching, praying, and listening, maybe it would not have taken this long. I know there's a message to be told–help to give someone along the way. I used to be bashful and now I talk too much. I know that some folks cry about different things that others may pray about or they wish they had. I learned to speak it into existence and pray about it or cry about it. Knowing how to live happily in this world is to know about our roots, our ancestors. We all need somebody to lead on. This is what makes the world a better place and the ups and downs are important. We have to go through much to become the people God wants,because if we all were perfect then we wouldn't be here. We would already be in heaven. You may think you need something to help you cope but it starts in your mind and if you don't let it through, then you'll be fine, listening to the right and not the wrong. Sometimes you can have so much blockage in your brain from your past that when something good comes along you may miss it.

Today I want to know how to thank Jesus Christ who saved my life. I want to know who I can tell this story to and I want to know who will listen. If I mentally go back to prison when I was locked up and realized that my kids were in prison too. I learned that all the bad you have done and gotten away with can make you feel important as life goes on. You may feel like you are the C.E.O.and have a PhD over drug war friends and you feel like you're on top of the world. Sometimes you may feel like you can fly, not realizing that you don't have wings.

I learned that it was only the devil and the devil is an addiction and you will pay the price because there will be a price to pay. Past lives matter and you were condemned repeatedly but remember to make the next generations better. Black lives matter because we have been stepped on for so long and are still being harmed by cycles of wrong. Start living up to the next generations and stop getting sucked into crime. Learn your inner self with peaceful thoughts and share in a peaceful way. Once you get in tune and listen, it's time to open up your mind and heart to live beyond the universe. Righteousness matters so listen before your actions. Pray for no mistakes and avoid wrong turns, because it's like fire: stop, drop and roll away from harmfulness.

Now I need to talk about how good God has been to me and what is the root, the reason or reasons for the matter. All the churches and all the schools saved me, along with family prayers. I learned to stop feeding that wrong Spirit that negatively impacts us—the one that grasped me and had a big hold on me. If you allow it, it will catch up with you and you will pay for it somewhere down the line. We all are born sinners and it starts from birth—being molested, raped, choked to death, or beaten by your mate. No one cared and evil grew up with me and no one was around to help.

Thinking about how you was raised and, with all those parents and all those siblings, you ended up a living reprobate. Practice having a forgiving spirit toward someone who wronged you so as to not hinder your prayers. It is better to go and reconcile with that person in Christ and pray later than to pray to God while bitterness is brewing in your heart. Miracles through God and believers with faith all start in the womb. My past life now focuses on my future and I know I'm far from living a perfect journey but this is a start because life is hardly ever what it seems and we've got to remember that we all are doing time. Everyone is on a clock and you never know your due date, because we all are born to die so help someone every day on their way.

First you are a child, and then a mother or father, and now a best friend. I thank God for my blessings and I pray that I can help someone along the way. I think and wonder how I got here and sometimes I ask myself where I am, but I learned to love the Lord with all of my heart, because praying really works.

I used to have a criminal mastermind, but I didn't use it to my advantage due to my addiction. If I knew now what I had then I would be well off, but it's never too late to utilize your capabilities. Now I just wanna say that I've been out there and it wasn't nothing nice and I should never have begun the streetwise crime games. You cannot be out there to waste time and if you chose the streets then you'll have to pay it off in pure bitterness, because the streets show no mercy. Out of foolishness I lived in the streets and I thank Jesus Christ that I didn't die in the streets. I'm not well yet but I know someone is watching over me. Thoughts are powerful and dreams are too; don't let no one take that away from you. I'm back at home and I'm trying so hard to connect with my children and they are so grown up.

My kids think that I love one of them more than the other but it's *never* ever like that. It's like everyone has a child out of their offspring that really looks up to you and you don't know and there's one in every family unless you only have one child. There's always one child that knows you better than the others. That same one will check your mistakes; that same one will respect you in spite of your wrongs; the same one will stand by your side at the end of the day and that one will not ask you for nothing and will tell you that they don't need nothing but your love and happiness. *I* thank God that I found myself before it was too late and I know Him. He is the one and the only one. If you don't have Him in your life, then you need to seek Him: Jesus Christ our Lord. PEACE! These are my miracles and this is my belief.

CPSIA information can be obtained
at www.ICGtesting.com
Printed in the USA
LVHW040842031120
670551LV00002B/205